Praise for *The Swelling Year*:

"It is good for the soul to notice the little things. It is even better to see them in the light of the big things. And Matthew Pullar does both in *The Swelling Year*, where his poems slow us down and help us to value our own mundane lives in the context of the drama of the church's year. For those with ears to hear, the Scriptures shout to us through these poems as we learn to listen to God afresh. And return to him the praise."

(Dr Rhys Bezzant, Ridley College)

"Poets have special gifts of seeing and saying. In these poems Matthew Pullar sees the words and works of God in the Bible, in human lives, and in our world, and he says what he sees with grace, insight, emotion, perception and power."

(Peter Adam, OAM, Vicar Emeritus of St Jude's Carlton, former Principal of Ridley College, and Canon Emeritus of St Paul's Cathedral)

Matthew Pullar has had poems published in Zadok Perspectives and in the 2018 anthology *Reaching for Mercy: Proost Poetry Collection 2*. He won the SparkLit Young Australian Christian Writer Award in 2013 for his unpublished manuscript *Imperceptible Arms: A Memoir in Poems*. He also regularly writes poetry, devotions and essays at his website, The Consolations of Writing. *The Swelling Year* was his first book of poems, first published in 2019, followed by *Les Feuilles Mortes* in 2020. Matthew is also joint poetry editor for Soul Tread Magazine. He lives in the western suburbs of Melbourne with his wife and their three sons.

anno domini

Poems and thoughts on a pandemic

Matthew Pullar

The poem "Anno Domini" was first published in *The Swelling Year*,
2nd edition, Consolation Press, 2020

*Sleepy riverside
in lock-down torpor,
people scattered like tumbleweed.*

***

*And when masks drop,
what smiles! What normality.
Yet every step a reminder
that all has changed.*

***

*Have we changed?
The river flows the same
but we must second-guess
even how we breath.*

"An isolated man is as such no man. 'I' without 'Thou'...is not human existence. Human being is being with other humans."

(Karl Barth, *God Here and Now*)

Plague Year

I.

It starts on a screen and you are immune:
so much begins and ends here, far away.
numbers alone are easy to reframe
and haven't we seen fears like this come and go?
Year begins in standard disarray;
wars and their rumours cycle just the same.
Tune in, tune out; everything's out of tune;
no time to heed the numbers as they grow.
You didn't catch the swine flu, and your plane
has never crashed. Daily life plays the odds
whatever you do. Only sometimes it's real
and the pinch you await to make you feel
awake again does not come. Sometimes God's
plans are to bring pride back to earth again.

II.

When lockdown began before Easter, we said
that life was teaching us Lent. We learnt how
to go without familiar things, to save
on toilet paper and bake Hot Cross Buns
with spelt, the only flour left in store.

Celebrations came and went; we planted
a vegetable garden, willed it to grow,
stewed quince ruby red, weathered the first wave
like a staying-home adventure, once
or twice fearing months of this, or more.

Slowly homes opened again; so did shops
and expectations. Spirits rose, numbers dropped.
Again we could dream our tentative dreams,
slowly dip back toes in ordinary streams.

III.

All this is hindsight which, as irony
would have it, is 20-20. Compared
with what came next, it seems bliss to have spent
our autumn watching leaves turn days on end,
to bake afternoon teas and to be spared
the contagion of crowds' anxiety.
In the early days, the rest was unknown:
the usual April sniffles threatened worse
things to come. Minds toyed with whether or not
it was better to just have it and be done
(for surely the healthy and youngish won't
have much to fear?). All this at first:
later we will have less vigour, more fear,
dreading what else might come to plague this year.

IV.

Like the hate. The ego that says, *Am I not
a living being?* The assertion of self.
The denial of neighbour. The mistrust.
The speed at which mind turns to conspiracy.
The black bile that spreads like a virus.
The will to be right. The assertion of right.
The hole at the centre turning to rot.
Oh the hate. The ego. The blindness of wealth.
The privilege of voice. The violence of spite.
The iron in the soul that turns to rust.
These plagues spread out where willing eyes can see.
The thought that soon we'll put all this behind us
belies the fond denials of the heart
that still will not admit it played its part.

July Diary

(1)

New world. Now the word "superspreader" is in our vocabularies. Now we watch the lists of suburbs in their second round of lockdown and wonder if we will be next. And once again the hoarders have begun to stockpile toilet paper, all circumstances that were utterly unimaginable even at the start of the year.

Yet it isn't all so strange for our species. I read today in Daniel Defoe's novel of the 1664 plague how people watched the death tolls in suburbs around them and wondered if they would be next; how people attempted to pinpoint where it came from, as though to find someone to blame; how people hid their symptoms to avoid being quarantined. And I'm reminded that humanity has known times like this more often than it has known the times of flourishing and health that we in the West take for granted.

It's the curious mixing of the familiar and unfamiliar in all of this that I want to capture: how quickly we can adjust to this "new normal" in some respects, even grow to quite like it, yet how surprised we can be by new manifestations of millennia-old vices and stains on our souls. I've caught myself in the past few days as I've waited on the results of my latest test (another new "normal") toying in my head with all the possible options: that I don't have the virus and will receive a text any minute now to reassure me; that I have it, and unknowingly infected all the guests at the 20-person wedding I attended on Saturday; that I have it, and caught it from someone at the wedding; that my whole family has it and have infected our friends; that we caught it from a friend. And as I play out each scenario I wonder which is best, as though there were a "best", an arrangement of facts that makes me least culpable or that would bring least shame on me; as though being sick in a time of global pandemic were somehow to fail, to be complicit in an evil. And I fear being the first in my group of friends, the first at my school, in my family, as though that would be "my fault" and I would have to bear the blame for all my loved ones who caught it from me. As though health were a virtue and sickness a sin best kept to oneself.

We talk more now than at any previous time in my living memory of being "all in this together", and in many ways it is true. The world is indeed unified by the experience: COVID-19 is no respecter of national or state borders, or of class divisions. Yet it also reveals our divisions more than ordinary life ever would. In my own city of Melbourne, we see how the majority of cases are clustered in less affluent areas. Globally we see how the already poor suffer worse than the rich, because health care is less developed or harder to access; because generations of entrenched poverty compromise immune systems; because it's hard to wash your hands regularly when you have no clean water; because it's impossible to socially distance in a refugee camp.

We also see how fear of contagion piggybacks on other fears: fear, in particular, of the Other. When the president of the USA calls it "the Chinese virus" and Chinese people are feared or despised for their country's involvement with the spread of the virus; when our neighbour coughing makes us suspicious; then we see our fears having more agency than our common bond. When family cannot meet across state boundaries, we see division trumping unity. And when we fear our countrymen and women over the border, we may "stay safe", but at the expense of what?

How hard to shift the focus from *what keeps me safe* to *what will most love my neighbour*. Harder still when our neighbours are required to stay behind their fences and we behind ours.

In our Father's house

Curtains are borders between me and the street.
Next door is an unseen checkpoint away;
other postcodes have police blockades
and I count the days until my home is the same.

By the bay we watch
numbers, statistics, localities named.
Quiet suburb whispers its fears.
No scapegoat to name, only

the innate mistrust of the island state
that says, "I choose who comes here."
How did this come here?
What conspiracy brings us cheek to cheek

with the airborne griefs that plague all humankind,
save us? This happens
only on TVs, never in 3d
where it reaches out with power to grab.

And does it console to know that,
somewhere, over oceans, others suffer
far worse than us? Hardly.
I must view you up close to take comfort in your distance.

When I open curtains, my neighbour crosses street,
crosses seas, to land at my doorstep, breathing,
"It's coming; you're next. The only place left
is our father's house, and we must share."

South

Waves pat the shore like an old friend.
Tucked in the bay, we gaze
from peninsula to peninsula,
and out through the heads to the sea.
My twin boys try to make
a swift getaway to Antarctica
and I, between moments of rush to pull them back,
breathe sea-breeze through my mask and see
the old familiar lapping of tides
and abide.
Nothing is known in this new tide,
but the only fixed point, whether ice should melt
and this island where I stand should fall to this sea,
is the firmness of grace as a rock beneath me.

July Diary

(2)

In the time since I started writing this, my whole city has been placed into lockdown, starting at midnight last night. I, like Defoe's narrator, had been watching the figures, seeing my municipality rise to be one of the most affected, expecting at least a local lockdown. Then there was the day of 200 cases and an emergency state cabinet meeting, after which all of Melbourne was given until midnight the following night to get our affairs in order before resuming Stage 3 lockdown restrictions. Schools would also be given an extra week of holidays for students, to give teachers like me a chance to prepare for a possible return to remote learning. Such a short time of being "outside" before the call to return to our homes. And so much harder to face the next six weeks, having begun to hope again that "normal" was returning.

I for one had been planning a trip that my family would take the coast during the holidays. I knew the streets we would walk, the beaches we would visit, the bookshops we would scour. We postponed the trip because I had to wait at home for the results of a test; and then the test results took a week, and then – the announcement that meant there would be no trip. Normal had evaded us again.

Yet what, we find ourselves asking, *is* "normal" now? Surely this is one of those times that the human psyche does not simply bounce back from, nor should it. In generations to come, we will no doubt have forgotten the enormity of the experience, the same way that we forgot the Spanish Flu until this year's events brought it back to public consciousness. But surely this generation will not forget easily? Surely we will always feel a degree of quiet gratitude when there's toilet paper on the shelves? Surely large gatherings will always feel at least a little unusual? Surely we will pay more attention to how carefully we wash our hands?

Some things we determinedly memorialise in our society. On Remembrance Day we are accustomed to hearing the words "lest we forget". Do we therefore need to remind ourselves of this time, in the years that hopefully lie ahead? Or will enough simply be forced to change forever that we won't need to remember? Will this whole time engrave itself upon our souls, like scars on once-infected lungs?

We still have the river

We still have the river, after it all,
running like a backbone though our home,
flowing sure when all else is gone;
we still have the river, still have the air.

We still have each other, at the end of the day,
grating on nerves, tired and numb,
still have our hearts beating together,
still have our days under the sun.

And when the river and the sun are gone,
when these days are over and done,
we'll still have the one who made rivers flow,
the Light before and after the sun.

Love

Yes, it takes our freedoms
because sometimes love does that:
for neighbour, for stranger,
for one who walks the same streets,
walks by your desk,
shops where you shop,
shares the same air.

Sometimes love lays down
rights - freedom of movement,
freedom of assembly,
freedom to smile and have others see -
because sometimes love judges
the more needful thing,
the truer way to be free.

Till We Have Our Faces Back

First you will learn about smiles,
how much you smile,
what's contained in a smile,
what's implied in the different degrees of smile:
in a curl of the lip at a funny thought,
in the mouth's outstretched corners
to greet the close acquaintance,
in the sardonic phrase,
the empathic moment.
All these things you will learn
when they cannot be seen.

And eyes. You will learn about eyes.
How readily you can recognise eyes
across a courtyard or carpark, how
much you can guess of a heart or a day
from the eyes poking out above the nose.

And breath. You will learn about breath.
You will taste it, smell it, absorb it all day.
You will choose your words and your silence to keep
moments when you can simply breathe.
You will long to stand
in the garden
beside your office
and do nothing
in that afternoon air
but take off your mask and breathe.

And faces - you will catch, in their absence,
the beauty, the wonder of faces,

the heart-catching, God-splendoured glory of faces.
You will long for the faces
that you loved and despised,
will search the room for these faces,
will wish that these faces
could transfigure their otherness straight into yours.
You will cover your face
and stifle your breath
and halve your smile
in hope of the day,
to work for the day,
when all of our faces are back.

July Diary

(3)

Certain events have the power to shift all human experience beyond that point. There was a profound difference between the world I grew up in and the world that emerged when I was seventeen and a plane crashed into the World Trade Centre. Likewise, we define many aspects of the twentieth century by their place in relation to the two world wars. Pre-war and post-war are different worlds. No-one can un-see a mushroom cloud. We cannot recover unthinking trust in the institutions that failed us in decades past.

So how will we characterise life before and after COVID-19? Will it be a blip on the human radar, or an irreversible shift like the jolt to the Earth's axis that the Fukushima earthquake caused?

The truth is, humans are prone to forget. The reason we continually make movies about the Nazi Holocaust or celebrate Remembrance Day is that we consider these to be matters worth keeping in the forefront of our consciousness. Otherwise, they might drift off into hazy antiquity, and we have collectively judged as a society that that must not happen.

So will we create ways of remembering COVID-19? Or will we be happy to forget it, the first moment that life affords us the luxury of doing so?

Quarantine Morning

What the day brings is anyone's guess:
Students in masks, temperature checks at the front gate,
But what else? Prognoses and rules change by the minute;
What yesterday was harmless today may destroy.
Brave new day that has such features in it.
And so, the day lying open
Like a box, like a question,
I rejoice to see vermilion horizon
That smiles on the locked-down and the risen alike.

Frontline: For the pandemic teachers

Check temperature before you leave;
Second guess that winter sniffle.

Hand-sanitiser with your markers,
Enter the ever-shifting classroom space.

Greet the students in masks.
Watch attendance, but don't be afraid.

Be calm. Reassure. You may mention the war
But know how to read the faces before you.

Keep life normal
When nothing is normal.

Plan.
(Nothing will go to plan.)

Admit when you are not okay
But face the battle nonetheless.

Adapt and keep
The children safe.

Breathe. Breathe. Breathe.

July Diary

(4)

This time will not remain in our memories the same way because it has not hit us all the same. Much as we have been united globally and nationally by this shared experience, it has met each of us in a way that has highlighted our differences as much as our commonality. While many of us have found a certain kinship on social media, sharing our stories of iso-baking or other new iso-hobbies, while we bond over the relatively common experiences of web conferences in pyjama pants or the challenges of doing anything socially meaningful via Zoom, these are experiences that point to privilege. Not all share them, though the narrative we co-construct as a society presents them as common to all. Not so. The tens of thousands infected now in Brazil are not just sitting at home baking sourdough. The clusters of cases in prison in the United States are not finding new hobbies. Those in refugee camps are not struggling with the lockdown blues like I am.

The differences are found even in the everyday details of people's lives in Australia. My friend who recently got married had to plan multiple different versions of her wedding as restrictions tightened then eased again. Her parents could not come from Malaysia to celebrate. My single friends have different experiences to my friends with children. My friends with reliable employment have not experienced the same anxieties as those who have been made redundant or who have had to suspend significant parts of their work for the foreseeable future. How I experience lockdown with my three children under three is unlikely to be altogether the same as how most of you reading this will have experienced it. And many Melburnians have been united recently in shared concern for the residents of our inner city housing commission towers, yet their experience of lockdown will be one of an intensity that I cannot imagine.

How we grieve this time looks different for the person who missed their long awaited holiday compared to the person who could not attend their grandmother's funeral, and how we struggle with isolation is different for the introvert who still loves people or the extrovert who struggles to manage the technology that will enable human contact. Much unites us, yet we vary in how we cope, and indeed in how closely we encounter the virus and its effects. Some may remember this as a time of minor inconvenience, while others will have been stripped of much of their security and normality. It hardly needs to be said that the latter will not bounce back like the former.

And how willing are we *to be changed* by our circumstances? While some might simply wait for it to end and others will be fighting to end it, some will also see in this a wake-up call to adjust priorities - a *memento mori*; a recognition that we are not in control. To be open to new ways of thinking in response to this time in no ways diminishes the horrors of how the virus has hit many; it is only a recognition that, when life fails to follow our expectations, we might be wise to review those expectations. Being unable to guarantee what I can buy from the shops week to week, for instance, makes me rethink what I *need* to buy. And being reminded that I am mortal is far from a bad thing; Psalm 90 associates "numbering our days" with applying our hearts to wisdom.

Merely waiting for this to end will mean that we live through one of the most significant experiences of recent human history and learn nothing from it. That might prove one of the greatest tragedies to emerge from it all.

5.

Why am I so uncomfortable with the government's latest advice, that we should wear facial masks when we go out? I react against anything that reminds me of dystopian fiction, fearful that I am living in an excessively sterile, disconnected society. Yet surely taking wise steps to protect yourself and the community seems the thing to do, however it might make me feel? Why, therefore, am I so unwilling to consider the prospect of teaching in a face mask? Removing the necessity of wearing the mask will only excuse me from asking what it is about myself and how I relate to other that the current circumstances might force me to confront. I would be wise to confront them thoughtfully.

Or why do we hoard? Why, more to the point, are people hoarding the second time around? Even though the only reason people ran out of toilet paper was the panic-buying that depleted stocks, nonetheless people are panic-buying again. And, while an end to the pandemic might take away the urge to buy apocalyptic levels of toilet paper, it would surely be informative if nothing else to inquire of our own hearts why we would ever be inclined to do such a thing.

And why the ennui? Fear we might understand, anxiety and depression too, but why boredom? Why do we turn to online shopping, to renovations, to writing operas or setting up YouTube channels? Why are we so afraid of being alone, of being still?

Extraordinary Time

Deprived of the ordinary markings of days -
drives to work, birthdays, people to celebrate -
we cling
more fervently to organic signs,
the constant shifts in the garden,
which trees have blossomed,
which ones have leaves,
how tall the pea plant has grown,
how white its petals.

These and the aphids signal time:
those and the snails migrating,
the worms beneath the compost,
the dead bird by the granny flat,
rising and falling daily tallies,
who died youngest, who's all clear
and how long until - we cannot say -
only greet other pilgrims on the way, and pray.

As yet untitled

As the changing but constant expectations
of a year that no-one chose keep knocking
and the day of the Lord lingers and tarries from my watch-post,
I long

to take this one quietly, on the bench,
with Saul and the others who couldn't run the race.
No shame in being worn out when
the swift themselves are flagging
and the flags
are all at half-mast or lower.
No prizes for laps of honour, least of all in a mask.
Preserve breath, preserve what
energy you have left, I say.

I say.
Though my words burn and I
would be better served not to speak
but to hear.
A voice like a whisper, like fire,
like a victor:
My yoke is easy. My burden is light.
No shoulders strong enough for burdens today;
even then, there is grace.

July Diary

(6)

Every day the landscape changes. Now Melburnians are glad when we have fewer than 200 new cases in a day, while Floridians try to find reasons why more than 15,000 new cases might not be as bad as it looks. Tomorrow I will have to take my temperature before I leave for work and email the office with my departure time and temperature. I will most likely have to teach in a mask. Today one newspaper published an article on the possible long-term health effects of the virus, even in those with mild cases, while another paper published an opinion piece on why multiculturalism in Melbourne is to blame for the spike. I cannot help but feel that we are living a reality now only seen previously in dystopian sci-fi. Yet every age since Jesus has believed itself to be close to the end, and many apocalypses have loomed with no result. What then? Do we ignore it all with ironic detachment? Do we simply wait for the storm to pass? Even if this apocalypse passed, the label may still be deserved. An apocalypse in the Greek sense is not a story of the world ending but a revelation. This is a time that is revealing much. Do we have eyes to see?

(7)

'We talk in the courtyards and corridors, under hushed breath and out loud, but not in the classrooms. In class, before our students, we enjoy something close to normal. But outside, we ask: How many cases today? Will it be over before they predicted? Will we all be home again soon? Did you have many students away today? Should we start teaching with masks? Maybe I shouldn't go to the shops on the way home.

(8)

My sister-in-law's school is closed for deep cleaning, and she and my in-laws must be tested because she had contact. "Getting tested", "school closure", "confirmed contact": all this shorthand that would have previously been meaningless. Our language too will bear the scars of this: words with dog whispers that we cannot unhear. Even my car registration looks like COVID to me when I view it from a distance. I cannot view this from a distance.

(9)

Just over a month ago, in Victoria the statistics looked like
this.

5th June - no new cases, no deaths
6th June - no new cases, no deaths
7th June - 4 news cases, no deaths
8th June - 2 new cases, no deaths
9th June - no new cases, no deaths
10th June - 4 new cases, no deaths
11th June - 8 new cases, no deaths
13th June - 4 new cases, no deaths.

This week in Victoria:
10th July - 288 new cases, no deaths
11th July - 216 new cases, one death
12th July - 273 new cases, one death
13th July - 177 new cases, no deaths
14th July - 270 new cases, two deaths
15th July - 238 new cases, one death
16th July - 317 new cases, two deaths
17th July - 428 new cases, three deaths

On the last day of the week, my 36th birthday awaiting on
Sunday, my temperature on arrival at school is 36. That's how I
will remember this birthday: the age of safe body temperature. God
willing. God willing it will stay safe.

God in all this

Our one desire and choice should be what is more conducive to the end for which we are created.
(St Ignatius of Loyola, *The Spiritual Exercises*)

Even this, Ignatius?
When all are in retreat in their homes,
when consoling and desolating spirits
vie for the attention of every moment,
when truth is in short supply
and what truth we have is despair,

even now
can we catch divine movement behind a face mask,
hear the Spirit call beyond garden walls,
see will and purpose despite ailing hope,
even now can we notice
Christ animate the soul
though it flags and fails?

Even now.

Anno Domini: For the Year 2020

"For he says, 'In a favorable time I listened to you, and in a day of salvation I have helped you.' Behold, now is the favorable time; behold, now is the day of salvation."
(2 Corinthians 6:2)

We did not choose you, would not repeat you.
Grief has built upon grief: ash and smoke first,
then this, a time we can only call
"unprecedented". And how it goes on.
How quickly "normal" becomes a word
stripped of all meaning. How quickly "Stay safe"
replaces "See you later". We saw none
of this coming. Jetpacks and life on Mars
were my childhood predictions, not this.
Yet future creeps up unannounced, and we,
had we heard her coming, would have moved to
Iceland, or bought shares in hand sanitizer.
Neither would we have chosen growth, or grace
bulldozing our plans and saving us instead.

July Diary

(11)

Last night, while reading a book that had nothing to do with any of this, I was shocked by the presence of the word *contact*. Then today, while watching television with my wife, I realised that I was squirming inwardly to see characters not physically distanced.

Even when we are talking about the virus, what we said a week ago seems quickly irrelevant or out-of-date. Today's count of new cases in Victoria - 217 - seemed mercifully small compared to yesterday's, yet it would have been the highest on record just over a week ago. The death count of 2 today does not sound terrible but only because we are immune to minor tragedy, having been inoculated by global disaster. A disease that kills a few Australians every day is nothing minor. And the truth is that scientists do not know the worst of it; survivors of minor cases, it seems, may be damaged in other ways despite avoiding death.

At the start of this month I asked the question of how we can shift from *what keeps me safe* to *what will most love my neighbour?* That question remains, yet it takes continual effort to keep it in the forefront of my mind. The ongoing mutations, the ever-shifting social and political landscape make it a daily task to keep abreast of the status quo. Tomorrow - my birthday - could bring realities that today are unimaginable.

Yet the question remains. How do I make this about loving my neighbour, not about keeping myself safe? In matters of pandemics, the two are not mutually exclusive. If I stay safe, I will not pass the virus on to anyone else. And I cannot catch the virus on behalf of anyone else, as if in catching it myself I spare someone else the suffering. Nor can I as a husband and father of three small children ignore the cost to others that my getting sick would cause. But loving my neighbour begins with me thinking of them when I read the news, and responding not with fear but with a readiness, an inclination to help or listen to the fears or vulnerabilities of others. It also means that, when - God willing it will be a matter of *when* - the virus leaves us, we do not become complacent but look for ways to help the nations that are still fighting it. It means smiling at the stranger walking past, while also stepping away to give them space to pass you. It means staying home when sick. It means wearing a mask when you don't want to. It means weathering this storm. It means guarding your heart so it can still be tender to love at the end of it all.

And when this is over - in a month or a year - it will mean a determination *not* to return to normal, because normal is complacent and love for neighbour cannot be complacent. It will mean remembering this time so that the sting of isolation does not leave us, so we can see it in the eyes of our neighbours and enemies and reach out to them as we have longed to be reached, with the joy of being able once again to reach out, of being able at last to smile with our masks gone.

Plague Year

V.

In my dreams now I see friends and hug them,
hold them tight for holding is what we lack.
Awake, I long to see below friends' eyes
but maskless I feel naked, incomplete.
At school I police smiles and proximity;
at home I long for distance to be null.
I count each kilometre between us;
I am weary to move, to venture from home.
Sky News and elections carve deeper rifts;
is there a body wide and riven enough
to span this abyss, to make home for scars?
Only one who has touched lepers, who lifts
the paralytic from the dirt. Only love
that gathers islands and scatters the stars.

Your Time is Not Our Time

Not only Chronos, the Titan,
youth-devouring Time,
not only the winged chariot
hurrying near,

not only the genial
Old Father Time,
the sluggish duration,
the waiting, the drag,

but also Kairos, Your time,
in compost and deadwood,
in premature ends
and abandoned beginnings,

here yet lingering,
growing fruit's potential
deep in soil, unseen,
    sure as sun.

July Diary

(12)

On my birthday Victoria recorded 363 new cases, the second highest number up to that point, and our Premier announced that masks would be mandatory from midnight on the following Wednesday. That was just over a week ago. Now, nearly a week into masks being a legal requirement, the internet floods with stories of a woman in Bunnings who refused to wear one and filmed herself protesting the rule, and we notice with a mixture of horror and anger those we encounter on the street or by the river who are not wearing theirs. And I have begun to adjust to teaching with a mask. Though teachers are not required to wear them while physically instructing a class, it seems wisest to me to do so. After all, the only times I come into contact with more people than when teaching are when I am at the shops. So I have slowly adjusted to the feeling of my glasses fogging up or of the shortness of breath that arises when I have been talking for a while. I am beginning to talk less, to conserve silence wherever I can. And conversely I am learning to wave at people I see instead of just smiling, or to say hello to strangers because otherwise we all look too dystopian for words.

Then today we read of the highest number of cases in a single day so far for Australia - 532. Yesterday we had our highest number of deaths in one day - 10. Figures that, when I began writing here, would have been utterly unthinkable.

And we cannot possibly know where it will end. I have returned continually to the question of how this pandemic will change us. Now I pray that we will survive it.

So how to end this diary? Being a diary, the story is unfolding before me, no hindsight. I could pause my writing and return later, when it has passed, but we have no way of knowing when that will be. Japanese writer Kenzaburo Oē visited Hiroshima decades after the bomb was dropped and reported in chilling detail the long-term cost of the bomb upon people born after the war. The effects of radiation on Chernobyl remain to this day, more than a generation after the explosion. We could be writing about the after-effects of COVID-19 well into this new decade and the ones that, God willing, will follow.

And I must finish now, because I am too tired of watching the numbers change and trying to capture the ever-evolving moment. I am tired, and I long simply to sit this out until it is over, to wake, like Rip Van Winkle, and find the war all finished with. I cannot do that, but I also can no longer make sense of what is happening.

What I can say is that there are now two prayers that resound in my heart, with increasing urgency and clarity. The first is, *What are you doing, Lord? Show us what you want us to learn.* The second is, *How long?*

Plague Year

VI.

We've been here before, so we hesitate.
How did it go last time? First tentative,
then slowly becoming gleeful - for some,
as though we never left. But then how quickly
we were back indoors, and worse than before.
And so - we hesitate, pausing in
the doorway to say, "Are we wearing masks?
We can if you want us to..." A new dance
as we carve new rules of decorum on
our still tender consciousness. Will we learn
the dance before it all changes again?
Will we learn polyrhythms for this time?
Fatigued from change, the broken soul suspects
the door we've stayed behind might still be best.

VII.

But we venture on. Newness at least is in
the air, on Capitol Hill, in the fruit
jumping out of trees. We cannot slow this
if we wanted to. Shopping aisles charge on
towards Christmas, while my heart craves Advent.
I could use the dark, the waiting, to bend
soul's joints back into shape, could use the long
silence to learn again to wait, to wish.
We have not yet traced the evil to the root,
nor will we. But our hearts may learn to sing
a purer song if they remember this:
the days we could not sing or hug or kiss,
the days we passed at home craving our home
where we'll no longer be apart, alone.

Turning

The scent was masked as we walked, though
hints of pollen pushed their way through cloth to me,
and on return
as I parked the pram and set
excited new walkers free to roam, I soaked
my senses in the radiance
of fruit trees delighting
in new white-pink growth,   and the hope
that if not now, soon at least,
signs are sure, sure to be
    soon.

Day Zero

Written on the first day that Melbourne recorded zero new cases or deaths in five months

On this day
I still wrestled my children
into their clothes,
still raced out the door
too late for comfort,
still pricked my finger with a rose thorn,

still feared that all my labour's in vain,
and found the evening slump
a little close to despair

yet
everything changed, while nothing changed
and mustard seeds of life were at work
whether we noticed
or not.

In Translation: After a psalm in Danish by N.F.S Grundtvig

The rhythms, in their consistency
feel trite.

My rhymes, to match his,
must become predictable, forced, as

though constraining to fit this neat,
Nordic order, when

nothing in this year
speaks of order.

Leave it so.
If it jars, let it:

I must be constrained
to the truth of grace, though

it marches on unbidden and I
feel a laggard in its wake.

Let me rush
to catch the pulsing of the constant rhyme

that I might find myself up-swept
in ever-flowing mercy,

breathless,
yet in time.

Welcome, God's year (Vær velkommen, Herrens år)

From the Danish of N.F.S Grundtvig
Translated by Matthew Pullar

Welcome, God's year,
And be welcome here.
On Christmas night, when the Lord was born,
A light came forth at the darkest dawn,
So welcome, new year. Welcome here.

Welcome, God's year,
And be welcome here.
On Easter Morning, when the Lord was raised,
The Tree of Life took root in the grave,
So welcome, new year. Welcome here.

Welcome, God's year,
And be welcome here.
On Pentecost Day, when God's Spirit came down to us,
Then down came His power, into our weaknesses,
So welcome, new year. Welcome here.

Welcome, God's year,
And be welcome here.
This now is God's year, filled up with God's favour,
New gladness is waiting in each day of God here,
So welcome, new year. Welcome here.

9 781716 437472